The Lord's Prayer for Children

Adapted from the King James Bible by Claire Abraham
Illustrated by Dean West

WestBow Press books may be ordered through booksellers or by contacting:

WestBow Press
A Division of Thomas Nelson & Zondervan
1663 Liberty Drive
Bloomington, IN 47403
www.westbowpress.com
844-714-3454

Scripture quotes are taken from the King James Bible,
Matthew 6: 9–13

Interior Image Credit: Dean West

ISBN: 978-1-6642-9995-5 (sc)
ISBN: 978-1-6642-9996-2 (e)

Library of Congress Control Number: 2023909696

Print information available on the last page.

WestBow Press rev. date: 5/31/2023

WESTBOW
PRESS®
A DIVISION OF THOMAS NELSON
& ZONDERVAN

Dedicated to the children of
St. Martin-in-the-Fields Episcopal Church,
Keller, Texas

Dear Father, who lives in Heaven,

Our Father which art in Heaven,

**We love your name
because it is special!**

Hallowed be thy name.

Help us to do what you want us to do,

Thy kingdom come, thy will be done,

Just like the angels do in Heaven.

On Earth as it is in Heaven.

Give us today the food we need,

Give us this day our daily bread,

Forgive us when we make mistakes,

Forgive us our trespasses,

**And help us forgive our friends
when they make us mad.**

As we forgive those who trespass against us.

Keep us away from bad choices,

Lead us not into temptation,

And help us to stay safe.

But deliver us from evil.

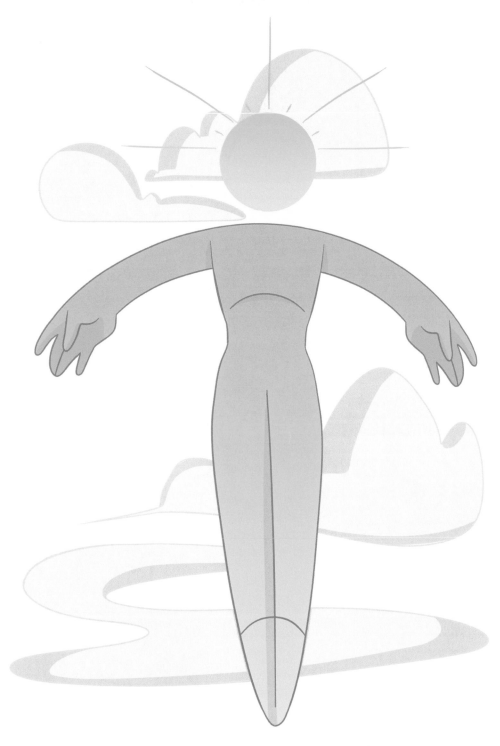

Because you are the King!

For thine is the kingdom, and the power, and the glory forever,

And we love you!

Amen.

Printed in the United States
by Baker & Taylor Publisher Services